Copyright:
© 2022
Charise Brown-Torres

All Rights Reserved.

My Experience
My Story
My Truth

Disclaimer: I am NOT a doctor, therapist, psychologist or any kind of medical professional.

I am someone that experienced negative things said to me often and I decided to share my story in this book I am UGLY. I share my experiences for you to be able to be comfortable enough to share your experience and know that you are not alone. Please pick up my book, the I am UGLY journal next and complete the fill in the blank options.

For a very long time, I believed what people said about me. I was convinced that they saw something I didn't see. Often, our perceptions are shaped by what others say. As children and teenagers, we listen to other people's opinions. That practice continues into adulthood and shapes who we think we are. Every comment dating back to childhood matters.

As a young girl,
I often heard adults
say things I didn't quite
understand, like "Respect
is due to a dog." Do we
respect our dogs?
I thought. The adults
taught me to respect my
elders and not talk back.
"Stay in a child's place
and out of grown folks'
business," they would say.
I was too young to question
what adults said, but I felt
awful about the things they
said about me.

I questioned myself, but I never questioned what they said. They were my elders, and they knew best, right? I just respected them and moved along because children believe the things adults say.

When I got older, that rule stuck with me. I never responded negatively to my elders, even if I felt disrespected. As I was taught, I replied with "yes ma'am" and "yes sir" and was sure to use Mr. or Ms. when addressing them.

The Power of Labels

Sometimes, other people's opinions become your reality. The things people say stick in your head and can even hurt your heart, especially when you're young and impressionable.

Ability

While some people can read instructions they are given, others benefit from a seeing a demonstration of how things should be done. Hearing directions was the easiest way for me to learn. My method of understanding instructions meant a label from adults—dyslexia.

Dyslexia is a learning disorder that affects your ability to read, spell, write, and speak.
In school, other students teased me because I didn't read as fast as they did.

9

Fortunately, I received positive feedback from special education teachers. They made sure I knew I was unique and intelligent and dispelled the claims from others that learning differently made me stupid.

Appearance

As a plus-size, brown-skinned girl, I was no stranger to people's opinions of me. "You're cute to be a plus-size girl" and "You're cute to be a brown-skinned girl," people would say. I was even called stupid more than once.

With the pseudo compliments looming, I started to believe what people said. I was under the impression that the color of my skin and my size made me cute. No one simply called me a cute girl. Would I have been just cute if I was light-skinned or petite?

As people critiqued my clothes and the things I said, self-doubt settled in. Some people don't realize how much harm their words can cause. Be mindful of the words you speak to children and young teens. Some may take things to heart. I know I did.

Awareness

People can label you however they want, but what matters is how you play into those labels and what you answer to. I had to realize that I was not stupid. I just learned things at a different pace. Just because it took me twice as long to read the book did not mean I was not intelligent.

Middle and high school were hard.
I participated in extracurricular learning and reading activities, but I didn't understand why. I didn't understand what dyslexia was.

I had to push past difficulties that I faced because of my appearance. Whenever I went out to bars and clubs with one of my close friends, the men would flock to her because she was smaller than me and her complexion was lighter than mine. In my eyes, she was always picked over me because she was prettier.

The men never sat down to get to know me for who I was. They took one look at me and skipped me. The men who approached me did so out of pity as I watched other men seek the attention of my friend. Luckily, I was smarter than they thought. Plus, I was gay, so I didn't want their attention anyway.

Affirmation

In relationships, my mates would tell me I was beautiful. Sometimes, I didn't believe them, but I'd respond with "ok" anyway. I had to make them understand that if I didn't feel it within myself, then I wouldn't believe I was beautiful.

As I got older, I learned the difference between what I saw and felt and what others saw and felt. I filled my tank with positive affirmations and surrounded myself with positive things.

In
those moments,
I learned who I truly
was. I sifted through
the lies I'd been
fed since childhood.
When I discovered
my
truth, the lies no
longer mattered.

Years ago, I participated in an online challenge. I wrote down all of the negative things I'd told myself over the years, tore the paper into pieces, and threw it away. It is important to get rid of all the negative things you've told yourself and heard from others.

A New Day

Everyone suddenly loved me when I lost 135 lbs. I was the new "it" girl. I heard compliments that were new to me: beautiful, pretty, gorgeous. I can assure you being congratulated for losing weight makes it feel like your greatest accomplishment, but it quickly confirms what you've feared all along.

It's sad that you have to be thin to be valued in this world. So many people told me how much older I looked when I was plus size.

They even told me that weightloss made my complexion lighter. I still wasn't as pretty as the others, though. Some of my friends with lighter complexions said they were bullied by brown-skinned girls who were jealous of their lighter, prettier appearance and wanted to scar their face.

In the African American community, some are ashamed of their skin color because of these very reasons today. Few of us are told we are beautiful no matter what.

This is my story and my truth. Perhaps you can relate to my experiences. Today, I feel like no one can define my beauty. As I tell my daughter daily, being pretty is just your outer appearance. Pretty clothes and makeup do not make you beautiful.

Those things simply enhance your beauty. True beauty comes from within. Having a nasty, disrespectful attitude makes you ugly. Being a good person is what counts. Your size and complexion do not matter. The positive, sweet, loving person on the inside matters.

I am U.G.L.Y.

Unique Gifted Lovable You

U Gotta Love Yourself

I am U.G.L.Y.

**UNIQUELY
GENUINELY
LOVING
YOURSELF**

Take Ugly as a compliment.

Negative Things...

I Used To Tell Myself...

Or Hear From Others...

You Are Worthless!

You Are Wor~~dl~~ess!

You Are Not Good Enough!

~~You Are Not Good Enough!~~

I Am Ashamed of Myself!

~~I Am Ashamed of Myself!~~

You Are Fat!

You Are Ugly!

You Are Ugly!

You Are Stupid!

~~You Are Stupid!~~

I Am A Failure!

~~I Am A Failure!~~

I Am A Loser!

~~I Am A Loser!~~

I Have Low Self-Esteem!

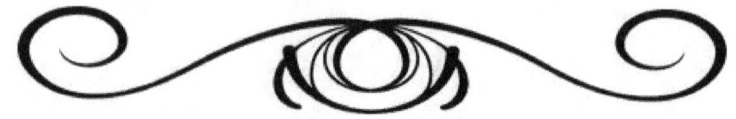

~~I Have Low Self Esteem!~~

You Don't Comprehend!

You Don't Comprehend!

I Am
Not
Loved!

I Am ~~Not~~ Loved!

You Are Not A Good Mother!

You Are Not A Good Mother!

You Will Never Amount To Anything!

You Will Never Amount To Anything!

This Is What I Tell Myself...

✗ Out
All Things
Negative...

Replace With All Things Positive…

Moving Forward!

I Will Love Myself For Who I Am & What I've Become!

My Problems Do Not Define Me!

I Am Beautiful Inside & Out!

I Am Smart!

always **DREAM** **BIG**

BE STRONGER Than Your EXCUSES

Be the person YOU WANT to have in Your LIFE

Be the reason someone smiles today

BECAUSE THIS IS MY LIFE and that's **THE ONLY** Explanation **YOU NEED**

Believe in yourself & you will be unstoppable

don't STOP UNTIL You're Proud

EVERY DAY IS
A NEW BEGINNING

take a deep breath

smile ☺

and (START) *again*

GET OUT OF YOUR OWN WAY

The Only Person you should try to be better than is the person you were yesterday

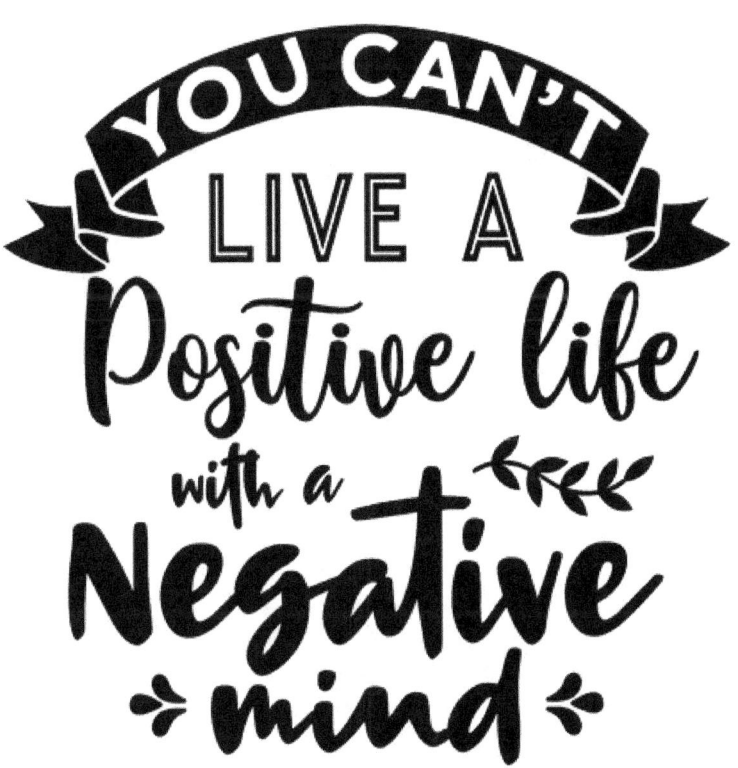

You don't
have to be
PERFECT
to be
Amazing

broken CRAYONS still color

www.ingramcontent.com/pod-product-compliance
Lightning Source LLC
LaVergne TN
LVHW021600070426
835507LV00014B/1878